CW01466500

FINLAND

[POCKET TRAVEL GUIDE]

Your Ultimate Guide to Nordic Adventures and Cultural Wonders

J.B TERRY

Copyright ©2024 by J. B Terry

All rights reserved. No part of his book may be reproduced or used in any manner without written permission of the copyright owner except for the use of quotations in a review.

FIRST EDITION FEB. 2024

MY AUTHOR CENTRAL

More of My Books from Here

TABLE OF CONTENTS

INTRODUCTION

Welcome, fellow adventurers, to the mesmerizing realm of Finland – a land where captivating landscapes, rich culture, and warm hospitality converge to create an unforgettable experience. As your trusted guide on this journey, I am delighted to invite you to delve into the wonders of Finland with me.

Finland, often hailed as the "Land of a Thousand Lakes," beckons with its pristine wilderness, vibrant cities, and timeless traditions. It is a place where ancient folklore meets modern innovation, where every forest holds a story, and every city corner reveals a piece of history.

In this meticulously crafted travel guide, we will embark on a voyage of discovery, peeling back the layers of Finland's enchanting tapestry. From the vibrant capital of Helsinki to the tranquil shores of the Archipelago, from the snow-covered expanses of Lapland to the bustling markets of Turku, each destination

offers a unique glimpse into the soul of this remarkable country.

But our journey extends beyond mere sightseeing – it is a chance to immerse ourselves in the essence of Finland, to connect with its people, and to experience its culture firsthand. From traditional saunas to mouthwatering cuisine, from lively festivals to serene moments in nature, Finland offers a wealth of experiences that will leave a lasting impression on your heart and soul.

So, dear travelers, prepare to be swept away by the allure of Finland as we embark on an adventure of exploration and discovery. Let us embrace the enchantment of this extraordinary land and allow ourselves to be captivated by its beauty, inspired by its culture, and enriched by its spirit. Together, let us unlock the secrets of Finland and create memories that will last a lifetime.

CHAPTER 1

BRIEF HISTORY AND CULTURE

GEOGRAPHY

Throughout its history, Finland has been shaped by a diverse array of influences, resulting in a rich tapestry of culture and tradition. Let's journey through time to uncover the key moments that have defined Finland's past and shaped its unique identity.

Ancient Roots: Long before recorded history, the land we now call Finland was inhabited by the indigenous Sami people. These resourceful nomads roamed the northern regions, relying on hunting, fishing, and reindeer herding for survival.

Swedish Dominion: In the 12th century, Finland came under Swedish rule, ushering in a period of cultural exchange and integration.

Swedish influence permeated Finnish society, introducing Christianity, agriculture, and governance systems. Over time, Finnish and Swedish cultures intertwined, giving rise to a distinct Finnish identity.

Russian Rule and Independence: In the early 19th century, Finland fell under Russian control following the Finnish War. Despite this, Finland retained a degree of autonomy and cultural independence, with the Russian Empire granting Finland the status of a grand duchy. Finnish nationalism flourished during this time, culminating in Finland's declaration of independence in 1917.

Cultural Renaissance: The early 20th century witnessed a resurgence of Finnish culture and identity. Artists, writers, and musicians embraced Finland's heritage, drawing inspiration from folklore, nature, and the national epic, the Kalevala. This cultural renaissance fueled a sense of pride and unity among the Finnish people, paving the way for Finland's emergence as a modern nation.

Contemporary Culture: Today, Finland is celebrated for its vibrant cultural scene, innovative design, and strong sense of community. Finnish culture is deeply rooted in nature, with outdoor activities like hiking, berry picking, and sauna bathing playing a central role in everyday life. Finland's rich artistic heritage is evident in its architecture, literature, and performing arts, showcasing a blend of tradition and modernity.

Geography

Finland's geography is as diverse as its culture, offering a stunning array of landscapes and natural wonders to explore.

Lakes and Forests: Finland is renowned for its vast network of lakes, numbering over 187,000 in total. These pristine bodies of water provide a tranquil backdrop for outdoor recreation and relaxation. Dense forests cover nearly three-quarters of Finland's land area, teeming with wildlife and offering endless opportunities for hiking, camping, and foraging.

Archipelagos and Coastlines: Along Finland's southern coast lies the stunning archipelago, a labyrinth of islands and rocky outcrops stretching out into the Baltic Sea. This unique maritime environment is a haven for birdwatchers, sailors, and nature enthusiasts, with charming coastal towns and villages dotting the shoreline.

Northern Wilderness: In the far north, Lapland beckons with its rugged mountains, vast tundra, and midnight sun. This pristine wilderness is home to indigenous Sami communities, who maintain a deep connection to the land through reindeer herding and traditional crafts. Lapland is also a popular destination for winter sports, with opportunities for skiing, snowboarding, and husky sledding abound.

Climate: Finland experiences a range of climates, from temperate in the south to subarctic in the north. Summers are mild and sunny, perfect for outdoor activities and festivals, while winters are cold and snowy, ideal for winter sports and northern lights viewing.

In summary, Finland's history and geography are intricately intertwined, shaping the country's cultural identity and providing a breathtaking backdrop for exploration and adventure. From ancient roots to contemporary culture, Finland offers a wealth of experiences for travelers seeking to discover its hidden treasures.

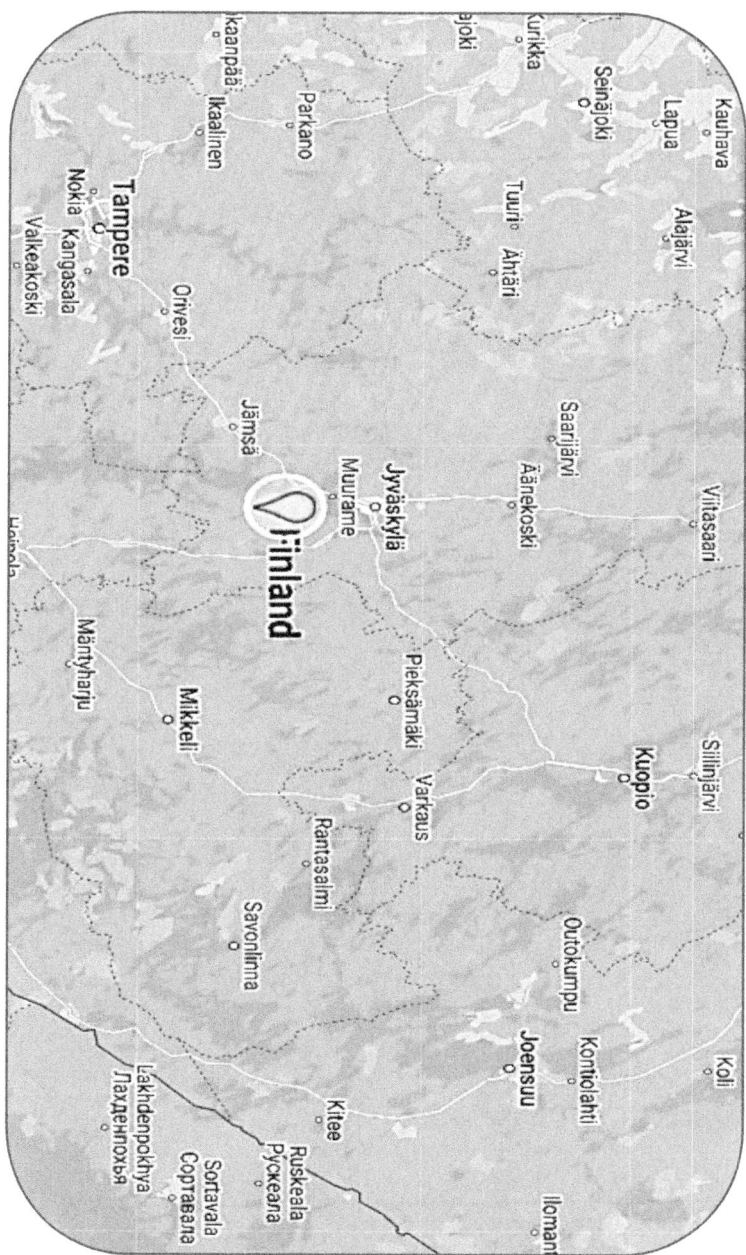

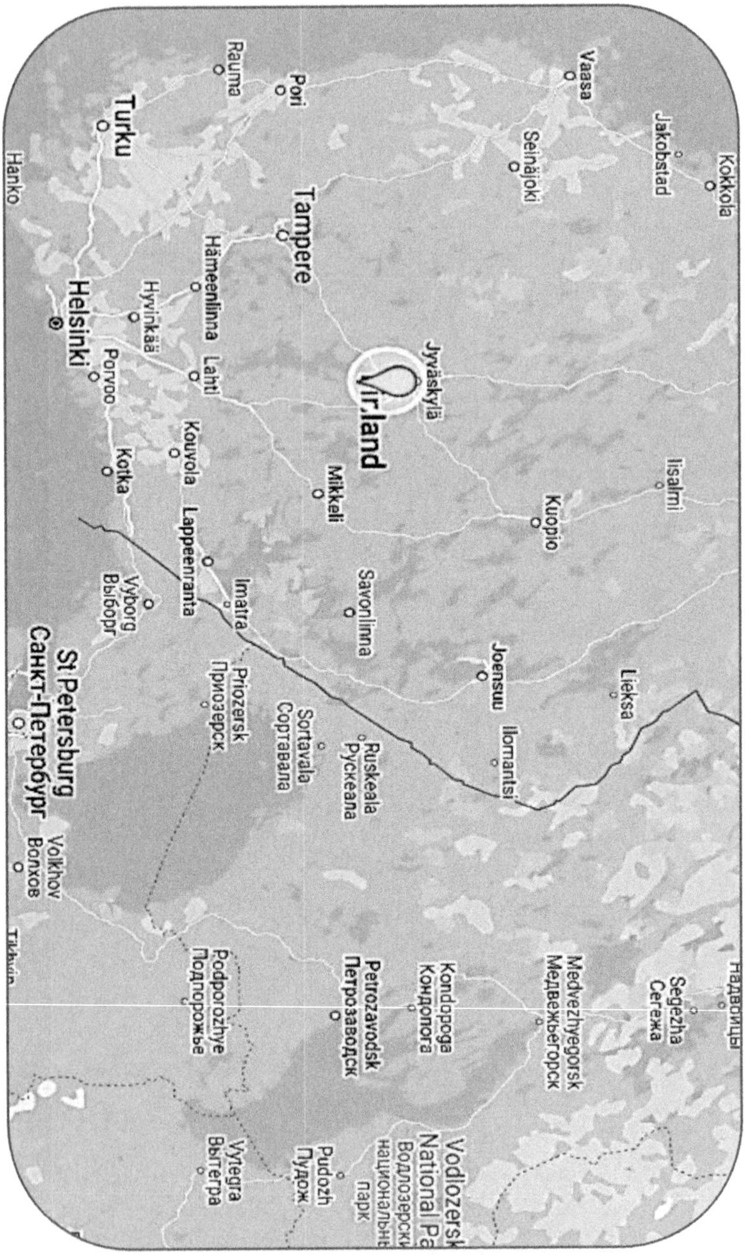
Vaasa
Jakobstad
Kokkola
Seinäjoki
Rauma
Pori
Turku
Hanko
Tampere
Hämeenlinna
Hyvinkää
Helsinki
Porvoo
Lahti
Jyväskylä
Finland
Kouvola
Kotka
Mikkeli
Iisalmi
Kuopio
Lappeenranta
Savonlinna
Imatra
Vyborg
Выборг
St Petersburg
Санкт-Петербург
Joensuu
Lieksa
Priozersk
Приозерск
Sortavala
Сортавала
Ruskeala
Рускеала
Ilomantsi
Volkhov
Волхов
Podporozhye
Подпорожье
Petrozavodsk
Петрозаводск
Kondopoga
Кондопога
Medvezhyegorsk
Медвежьегорск
Segezha
Сегежа
Надвоицы
Vytegra
Вытегра
Pudozh
Пудож

CHAPTER 2

FUN FACTS ABOUT FINLAND

1. **Land of a Thousand Lakes:** Finland is often referred to as the "Land of a Thousand Lakes," but in reality, it boasts over 187,000 lakes, making it one of the most lake-dense countries in the world. These pristine bodies of water offer endless opportunities for swimming, boating, and fishing.

2. **Sauna Capital of the World:** Finland is renowned for its sauna culture, with an estimated 3.3 million saunas for a population of 5.5 million people. Saunas hold a special place in Finnish culture, providing a relaxing and rejuvenating experience for both body and mind.

3. **Midnight Sun and Polar Nights:** In the northernmost regions of Finland, the sun does not set for several weeks during the summer months, a phenomenon known as the "midnight sun." Conversely, during the winter months, the sun remains below the horizon for an extended period, creating the magical "polar nights."

4. **Home of Santa Claus:** The Finnish town of Rovaniemi, located in Lapland, is known as the official hometown of Santa Claus. Visitors can meet Santa year-round at Santa Claus Village, where they can

tour his workshop, send letters, and even cross the Arctic Circle.

5. **Innovative Education System:** Finland's education system is consistently ranked among the best in the world. Finnish schools emphasize creativity, critical thinking, and equal opportunities for all students, with minimal standardized testing and homework.

6. **Heavy Metal Capital:** Despite its peaceful reputation, Finland has a thriving heavy metal music scene and boasts more heavy metal bands per capita than any other country in the world. The annual Tuska Open Air Metal Festival in Helsinki attracts metalheads from around the globe.

7. **Berry Picking Tradition:** Berry picking is a beloved Finnish pastime, with locals venturing into the forests to forage for

wild berries during the short but bountiful summer months. Popular berries include lingonberries, blueberries, and cloudberries, which are used in various culinary dishes and desserts.

8. **Gender Equality:** Finland is consistently ranked as one of the most gender-equal countries in the world. Women hold prominent positions in government, business, and academia, and gender equality is enshrined in Finnish law and society.

9. **National Emojis:** Finland became the first country in the world to release its own set of national emojis, showcasing iconic Finnish symbols and cultural references. From sauna emojis to the iconic Moomin characters, these emojis capture the essence of Finnish culture in a playful and creative way.

10.   **Ice Swimming Tradition:** Ice swimming is a popular winter activity in Finland, with brave souls taking a dip in icy waters for health and relaxation. Many Finns believe that ice swimming boosts immunity, improves circulation, and enhances overall well-being.

Tips you should

1. **Respect Sauna Etiquette:** When visiting a sauna in Finland, it's essential to respect sauna etiquette. Always shower before entering the sauna, sit or lay on a towel, and refrain from loud conversation. If you're not sure, follow the locals' lead.

2. **Embrace the Midnight Sun:** If you're visiting Finland during the summer months, embrace the phenomenon of the midnight sun. Take advantage of the extended daylight hours by exploring the

outdoors late into the evening and experiencing the magic of the never-ending daylight.

3. **Dress for the Weather:** Finland's weather can be unpredictable, so it's essential to dress appropriately for the season. In winter, bundle up in layers and don't forget a warm hat, gloves, and sturdy boots. In summer, lightweight, moisture-wicking clothing is key, along with sunscreen and sunglasses.

4. **Learn Some Finnish Phrases:** While many Finns speak English fluently, learning a few basic Finnish phrases can go a long way in showing respect and appreciation for the local culture. Simple greetings like "kiitos" (thank you) and "moi" (hello) are always appreciated.

5. **Try Traditional Finnish Cuisine:** Don't leave Finland without sampling some

traditional Finnish dishes. From creamy salmon soup and hearty reindeer stew to sweet cinnamon buns and cloudberries, Finnish cuisine offers a delightful array of flavors and tastes.

6. **Take Advantage of Public Transportation:** Finland boasts an efficient and reliable public transportation system, including trains, buses, and ferries. Consider purchasing a regional travel pass for unlimited travel within a specific area, or opt for a multi-day train pass for exploring the country.

7. **Respect Nature:** Finland's pristine wilderness is a treasure to be protected and preserved. When exploring nature, always follow Leave No Trace principles, stay on designated trails, and avoid disturbing wildlife. Remember to pack out

any trash and leave the environment as you found it.

8. **Experience the Northern Lights:** If you're visiting Finland during the winter months, don't miss the opportunity to witness the mesmerizing northern lights. Head to a dark, remote location away from city lights for the best chance of seeing this natural phenomenon.

9. **Participate in Outdoor Activities:** Finland offers a wide range of outdoor activities year-round, from skiing and snowboarding in winter to hiking and berry picking in summer. Embrace the Finnish love of nature by participating in outdoor adventures suited to your interests and abilities.

10. **Enjoy Finnish Hospitality:** Above all, enjoy the warm hospitality of the Finnish people. Whether you're staying in

a cozy cottage in the countryside or exploring the bustling streets of Helsinki, you'll find that Finns are friendly, welcoming, and always ready to share their culture with visitors.

Things you should avoid

1. **Disrespecting Sauna Etiquette:** Saunas hold a special place in Finnish culture, so it's essential to respect sauna etiquette. Avoid loud conversations, excessive splashing, or other disruptive behavior that may disturb others in the sauna.

2. **Underestimating the Weather:** Finland's weather can be unpredictable, especially during the winter months. Avoid being caught unprepared by checking the weather forecast regularly and dressing appropriately for the

conditions. Don't underestimate the cold and always wear layers to stay warm.

3. **Ignoring Wildlife Guidelines:** Finland is home to diverse wildlife, including bears, wolves, and lynx. When exploring nature, avoid approaching or feeding wild animals, as this can be dangerous for both you and the animals. Respect wildlife habitats and keep a safe distance when observing animals.

4. **Disregarding Personal Space:** Finns value their personal space and privacy, so it's important to respect boundaries when interacting with locals. Avoid standing too close or engaging in overly familiar behavior, especially with strangers.

5. **Being Late:** Punctuality is highly valued in Finnish culture, so avoid being late for appointments, meetings, or social gatherings. Arrive on time or a few minutes early to show respect for others' time and schedules.

6. **Disrespecting Nature:** Finland's natural environment is fragile and should be treated with care and respect. Avoid littering, damaging vegetation, or disturbing wildlife when exploring outdoor spaces. To reduce your environmental impact, stay on designated trails and follow Leave No Trace principles.

7. **Overindulging in Alcohol:** While Finns enjoy their drinks, excessive alcohol consumption is generally frowned upon. Pace yourself when drinking and avoid becoming intoxicated, especially in public places. Drinking responsibly ensures a safe and enjoyable experience for everyone.

8. **Ignoring Cultural Norms:** Finland has its own unique cultural norms and customs, so take the time to familiarize yourself with them before visiting. Avoid behaviors that may be considered rude or offensive, such as talking loudly in public places or interrupting others while they're speaking.

9. **Disrespecting Silence:** Finns value silence and tranquility, especially in nature. Avoid making unnecessary noise or disturbing the peace when outdoors.

Take the time to appreciate the natural surroundings and embrace moments of quiet reflection.

10.   **Overlooking Local Cuisine:**

Finnish cuisine may not be as well-known as some other European cuisines, but it offers a delicious array of flavors and dishes to explore. Avoid sticking to familiar foods and be adventurous by trying traditional Finnish dishes like reindeer stew, smoked salmon, and Karelian pastries.

Languages spoken in the Finland

1. **Finnish:** Finnish is the official language of Finland and is spoken by the majority of the population. It belongs to the Finno-Ugric language family and has a reputation for its complex grammar and vowel harmony system. Finnish is written using the Latin alphabet with a few additional letters, such as ä, ö, and å.

2. **Swedish:** Swedish is the second official language of Finland and is spoken primarily in the coastal regions of western and southern Finland, as well as in the autonomous region of Åland. Swedish-speaking Finns make up about 5-6% of the total population. Swedish is also taught as a second language in Finnish schools, making it widely understood throughout the country.

3. **Sami Languages:** The Sami languages are a group of indigenous languages spoken by the Sami people in northern Finland, as well as in Norway, Sweden, and Russia. There are several Sami languages, including Northern Sami, Inari The majority of Finland's population speaks Finnish, which is the country's official language. The majority of Finland's population speaks Finnish, which is the country's official language. Sami, and Skolt Sami. These languages are considered endangered and efforts are being made to preserve and revitalize them.

4. **Russian:** Due to Finland's proximity to Russia and historical ties with the country, Russian is spoken by a small percentage of the population, particularly in border areas and among Russian-speaking

immigrants. Russian is also taught as a second language in Finnish schools.

5. **English:** English is widely spoken and understood in Finland, particularly among younger generations and in urban areas. It is taught as a mandatory subject in Finnish schools from an early age, and many Finns are proficient in English, making it easy for visitors to communicate with locals.

Phrases for travel

1. **Hello/Hi**: "Hei" (pronounced hey) - A common and informal way to greet someone in Finnish.

2. **Goodbye**: "Näkemiin" (pronounced nah-keh-meen) - Used to say goodbye when leaving.

3. **Thank you**: "Kiitos" (pronounced kee-tohss) - A polite way to express gratitude.

4. **Please**: "Ole hyvä" (pronounced oh-leh huu-vaa) - Used to politely ask for something or to indicate politeness.

5. **Excuse me**: "Anteeksi" (pronounced ahn-tehk-see) - Used to get someone's attention or to apologize for accidentally bumping into someone.

6. **Do you speak English?**: "Puhutteko te englantia?" (pronounced poo-huht-teh-koh teh ehn-glahn-tee-ah) - Useful for asking if someone speaks English.

7. **I don't understand**: "En ymmärrä" (pronounced en uhm-maar-uh) - Useful for indicating that you don't understand something.

8. **Where is...?**: "Missä on...?" (pronounced mees-sa ohn) - Use this phrase followed by the place or location you are looking for.

9. **How much does it cost?**: "Paljonko se maksaa?" (pronounced pahl-yohn-koh seh mahk-sah-ah) - Useful for asking about prices when shopping or dining.

10. **Can you help me?**: "Voitteko auttaa minua?" (pronounced voy-teh-koh ow-tah mih-noo-ah) - Used to ask for assistance or directions.

Remember to speak slowly and clearly when using these phrases, and don't be afraid to use gestures or simple drawings to help communicate if necessary. Most Finns appreciate the effort to speak their language, even if it's just a few words.

CHAPTER 3

BEST TRAVEL SEASON

The best travel season in Finland largely depends on your interests and what you hope to experience during your visit. Here's a breakdown of the seasons and what they offer:

1. **Summer (June to August):**

    - Summer is the most popular time to visit Finland, thanks to its long daylight hours and mild weather.

    - During the summer months, you can experience the phenomenon of the midnight sun, where the sun doesn't set for several weeks in the northern regions.

- Summer is ideal for outdoor activities such as hiking, biking, fishing, and kayaking. The countryside is lush and green, and the lakes are perfect for swimming and boating.

- Additionally, summer is festival season in Finland, with numerous music, arts, and cultural festivals taking place throughout the country.

2. **Autumn (September to November):**

- Autumn in Finland is a magical time when the landscape transforms into a riot of vibrant colors as the leaves change.

- This is a great time for nature lovers and photographers, as the forests and countryside are ablaze with hues of red, orange, and gold.

- Autumn is also the season for berry and mushroom picking, with abundant opportunities to forage for wild berries and mushrooms in the forests.

3. **Winter (December to February):**

- Winter transforms Finland into a winter wonderland, with snow-covered landscapes and opportunities for winter sports and activities.

- Lapland, in particular, is a popular destination for winter enthusiasts, offering activities such as skiing, snowboarding, snowmobiling, and husky sledding.

- Winter is also the best time to experience the magical northern lights, with clear, dark nights providing optimal viewing conditions.

- Additionally, winter in Finland is synonymous with Christmas markets, where you can shop for handmade crafts, sample traditional Finnish foods, and soak up the festive atmosphere.

4. **Spring (March to May):**

- Spring marks the awakening of nature in Finland, with the melting snow giving way to blooming flowers and budding trees.

- This is a great time for outdoor activities such as birdwatching, hiking, and wildlife spotting, as the countryside comes to life with the arrival of migratory birds and other wildlife.

- Spring is also the season for "ruska," or the Finnish version of "fall foliage," as the landscape transitions from winter to summer, offering stunning views of the changing colors.

Overall, the best time to visit Finland depends on your interests and what you hope to experience during your trip. Whether you're seeking outdoor adventures, cultural festivals, or the beauty of nature in its various seasons, Finland has something to offer year-round.

Navigating Finland: Tips for Getting Around

1. **Public Transportation:**

   - Finland boasts an efficient and reliable public transportation system, including trains, buses, trams, and ferries.

- Helsinki, the capital city, has an extensive network of trams and buses, making it easy to navigate the city center and surrounding areas.

- For longer distances, consider taking the train, which connects major cities and towns across the country. The Finnish railway system is known for its punctuality and comfort.

2. **Renting a Car:**

- Renting a car is a convenient option for exploring rural areas and off-the-beaten-path destinations in Finland.

- Roads in Finland are well-maintained and well-signposted, making driving relatively easy for visitors.

- Keep in mind that Finland has strict regulations regarding winter driving, including mandatory winter tires and, in some cases, the use of snow chains.

3. **Cycling:**

- Cycling is a popular mode of transportation in Finland, especially in urban areas and during the warmer months.

- Many cities in Finland have designated bike lanes and bike-sharing programs, making it easy to rent a bike and explore the city on two wheels.

- For longer cycling trips, consider exploring one of Finland's many scenic cycling routes, such as the Archipelago Trail or the King's Road.

4. **Walking:**

- Finland is a pedestrian-friendly country, with well-maintained sidewalks and pedestrian crossings in urban areas.

- Walking is an excellent way to explore Finland's cities and towns, allowing you to soak up the atmosphere and discover hidden gems at your own pace.

- In rural areas and national parks, hiking trails offer opportunities for scenic walks and outdoor adventures amidst Finland's breathtaking landscapes.

5. **Domestic Flights:**

- For travelers short on time or looking to cover long distances quickly, domestic flights are available between major cities in Finland.

- Finnair, the national airline, operates flights to numerous destinations within Finland, including Helsinki, Rovaniemi, and Oulu.

- Keep in mind that flying within Finland may be more expensive than other forms of transportation, so be sure to compare prices and book in advance when possible.

6. **Boating and Ferries:**

- With its extensive coastline and numerous lakes, boating and ferry travel are popular ways to explore Finland's waterways.

- Ferries connect Finland's coastal cities and islands, offering scenic views and opportunities to experience Finland's maritime culture.

- Additionally, boat tours and cruises are available on Finland's lakes and rivers, providing a unique perspective on the country's natural beauty.

Overall, navigating Finland is relatively easy, thanks to its well-developed transportation infrastructure and pedestrian-friendly cities. Whether you're traveling by public transportation, car, bike, or on foot, Finland offers a variety of options for exploring its diverse landscapes and vibrant cities.

CHAPTER 4

WHAT TO PACK

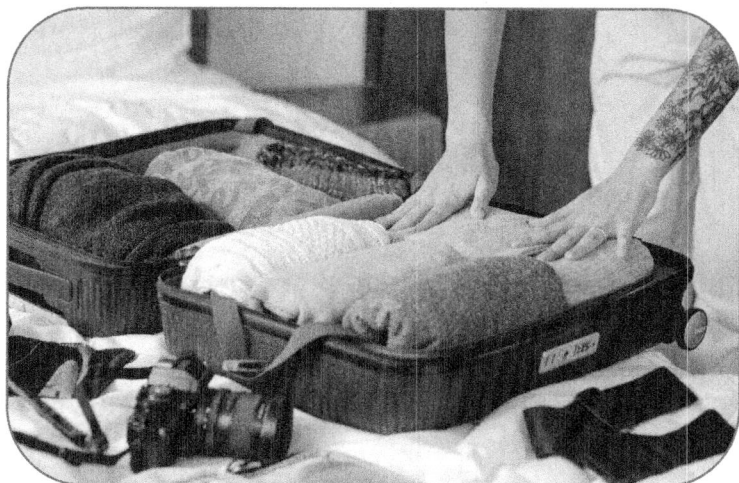

1. **Clothing:**

- **Layers:** Finland's weather can be unpredictable, so pack clothing that can be layered for warmth and versatility. Include items like long-sleeved shirts, sweaters, and a waterproof jacket.

- **Winter Gear:** If you're visiting in the colder months, don't forget essentials like a warm coat, insulated boots, hats, gloves, and scarves. Thermal underwear and wool socks are also recommended for extra warmth.

- **Comfortable Shoes:** Whether you're exploring cities or hiking in the wilderness, comfortable and sturdy shoes are a must. Opt for waterproof footwear to keep your feet dry in wet conditions.

- **Swimwear:** If you're visiting during the summer months, pack swimwear for enjoying Finland's lakes and saunas.

2. **Outdoor Gear:**

- **Daypack:** A small backpack or daypack is handy for carrying essentials like water, snacks, sunscreen, and a camera while exploring Finland's outdoors.

- **Hiking Gear:** If you plan on hiking, pack appropriate gear such as a sturdy backpack, hiking boots, trekking poles, and a map or GPS device. Don't forget to check the weather forecast and pack accordingly.

- **Binoculars:** Finland is home to diverse wildlife, so bring binoculars for birdwatching or wildlife spotting opportunities.

3. **Travel Accessories:**

- **Travel Adapter:** Finland uses Type C and Type F electrical outlets, so bring a travel adapter to ensure you can charge your electronic devices.

- **Reusable Water Bottle:** Finland's tap water is safe to drink, so bring a reusable water bottle to stay hydrated while reducing plastic waste.

- **Travel Wallet:** Keep your important documents, such as passport, ID, credit cards, and cash, organized and secure in a travel wallet or pouch.

- **First Aid Kit:** Pack a basic first aid kit with essentials like bandages, antiseptic wipes, pain relievers, and any prescription medications you may need.

4. **Personal Items:**

- **Toiletries:** Pack travel-sized toiletries such as shampoo, conditioner, body wash, toothpaste, and sunscreen. Don't forget items like a toothbrush, razor, and any personal hygiene products you may need.

- **Medications:** Bring any prescription medications you require, as well as over-the-counter medications for common ailments like headaches, allergies, and stomach upset.

- **Travel Documents:** Don't forget to bring essential travel documents such as your passport, travel insurance information, itinerary, and any necessary visas or permits.

5. **Miscellaneous:**

- **Guidebook or Map:** Bring a guidebook or map to help navigate Finland's cities, towns, and attractions. Alternatively, download offline maps or use a GPS navigation app on your smartphone.

- **Reusable Bags:** Reduce plastic waste by bringing reusable bags for shopping and carrying souvenirs.

- **Snacks:** Pack snacks like granola bars, nuts, and dried fruit for on-the-go energy during long days of exploring.

By packing these essentials, you'll be well-prepared for your adventure in Finland, whether you're exploring cities, hiking in the wilderness, or relaxing by the lakeside.

What to wear

1. **Layers:**
   - Finland's weather can vary widely depending on the season, so dressing in layers is key. Start with

a base layer such as a lightweight shirt or thermal underwear, add a mid-layer like a sweater or fleece, and top it off with a waterproof jacket or coat.

2. **Winter Clothing:**

- If you're visiting Finland in the winter months (December to February), be sure to pack warm clothing to stay comfortable in the cold temperatures. This includes a heavy coat or parka, insulated boots, thermal underwear, hats, gloves, and scarves.

3. **Summer Clothing:**

- In the summer months (June to August), Finland experiences milder temperatures, but it's still a good idea to pack lightweight and breathable clothing. Consider packing shorts, T-shirts, lightweight pants or skirts, and a light jacket or sweater for cooler evenings.

4. **Footwear:**

- Regardless of the season, comfortable and sturdy footwear is essential for exploring Finland. In winter, opt for insulated boots with good traction to navigate snowy and icy conditions. In summer, lightweight hiking shoes or sandals are suitable for outdoor activities.

5. **Rain Gear:**

- Finland is known for its unpredictable weather, so it's wise to pack rain gear such as a waterproof jacket, pants, and umbrella. This will keep you dry and comfortable during sudden rain showers or inclement weather.

6. **Accessories:**

- Don't forget to pack accessories to protect yourself from the elements. In winter, this may include a warm hat, gloves, and a scarf to keep you insulated against the cold. In summer, sunglasses, sunscreen, and a wide-brimmed hat are essential for sun protection.

7. **Indoor Attire:**

- If you plan on visiting museums, restaurants, or other indoor attractions, it's a good idea to pack some slightly dressier clothing. This could include casual dresses, slacks, blouses, or button-up shirts for a smart-casual look.

8. **Swimwear:**

- Finland is home to thousands of lakes and saunas, so don't forget to pack swimwear if you plan on taking a dip or enjoying a traditional Finnish sauna experience.

9. **Mosquito Repellent:**

- In the summer months, especially in rural areas and near bodies of water, mosquitoes can be quite prevalent. Be sure to pack mosquito repellent to ward off these pesky insects and avoid uncomfortable bites.

By packing a variety of clothing options suitable for different weather conditions, you'll be prepared to enjoy all that Finland has to offer, whether you're exploring cities, hiking in the wilderness, or relaxing by the lakeside.

CHAPTER 5

MUST-SEE ATTRACTIONS

1. Helsinki:

- Explore the vibrant capital city of Helsinki, known for its stunning architecture, bustling markets, and rich cultural scene. Don't miss iconic landmarks such as the Helsinki Cathedral, Suomenlinna Sea Fortress, and Temppeliaukio Church (Rock Church).

2. Northern Lights:

- Head to the northern regions of Finland, such as Lapland, during the winter months for a chance to witness the mesmerizing northern lights (aurora borealis) dance across the night sky.

3. **Santa Claus Village:**

- Visit the official hometown of Santa Claus in Rovaniemi, Lapland. Meet Santa himself, cross the Arctic Circle, and explore the festive atmosphere of this magical winter wonderland.

4. **Lakes and Archipelagos:**

- Discover Finland's natural beauty by exploring its countless lakes and picturesque archipelagos. Take a boat cruise, go kayaking, or simply relax by the water's edge and soak in the serene surroundings.

5. **National Parks:**

- Experience Finland's pristine wilderness by visiting one of its many national parks. Highlights include Urho Kekkonen National

Park, Nuuksio National Park, and Lemmenjoki National Park, where you can hike, camp, and spot native wildlife.

6. **Rovaniemi Arctic Wildlife Park:**

- Get up close and personal with Finland's native wildlife at the Rovaniemi Arctic Wildlife Park. Encounter reindeer, moose, bears, and other Arctic animals in their natural habitats.

7. **Moomin World:**

- Step into the whimsical world of the Moomins at Moomin World in Naantali. This theme park based on the beloved Finnish children's books features Moomin-themed attractions, performances, and activities for the whole family to enjoy.

8. Linnanmäki Amusement Park:

- Have a fun-filled day at Linnanmäki Amusement Park in Helsinki. With thrilling rides, games, and entertainment for all ages, it's a must-visit attraction for families and thrill-seekers alike.

9. Kalevala Village:

- Immerse yourself in Finnish folklore and culture at Kalevala Village in Kuhmo. Explore traditional wooden buildings, learn about ancient Finnish mythology, and experience authentic Sami culture.

10. Husky Safari:

- Embark on a husky safari through Finland's snowy wilderness for an unforgettable adventure. Let a team of eager huskies pull you through the snow-covered landscapes of Lapland, taking in the stunning scenery along the way.

These are just a few of the many incredible attractions waiting to be explored in Finland. Whether you're interested in nature, culture, or adventure, Finland offers something for every traveler to enjoy.

Exciting Activities to Enjoy in Finland

1. Husky Sledding:

- Experience the thrill of being pulled by a team of huskies through Finland's snowy landscapes. Husky sledding tours are available in Lapland and other northern regions, offering an unforgettable adventure for all ages.

2. Northern Lights Hunting:

- Embark on a magical journey to witness the enchanting northern lights dance across the Arctic sky. Join guided tours led by knowledgeable locals who will take you to the best viewing spots for optimal aurora sightings.

3. **Sauna Experience:**

- Immerse yourself in Finland's rich sauna culture by indulging in a traditional sauna experience. Whether in a lakeside cottage, urban spa, or remote wilderness retreat, the Finnish sauna ritual is a must-try for visitors.

4. **Snowshoeing and Cross-Country Skiing:**

- Explore Finland's winter wonderland on snowshoes or cross-country skis. Traverse snow-covered forests, frozen lakes, and scenic trails while enjoying the tranquility of the snowy landscapes.

5. **Reindeer Safaris:**

- Embark on a reindeer safari and learn about the traditional Sami way of life. Ride in a traditional reindeer sled through Lapland's snowy wilderness and gain insight into the cultural significance of reindeer herding.

6. **Ice Fishing:**

- Experience the thrill of ice fishing on Finland's frozen lakes and rivers. Join local guides who will teach you the art of drilling through the ice, setting up fishing lines, and catching fish beneath the icy surface.

7. **Midnight Sun Activities:**

- Make the most of Finland's long summer days by engaging in outdoor activities under the midnight sun. From hiking and biking to kayaking and fishing, there are endless opportunities to enjoy the great outdoors in the land of the midnight sun.

8. **Wildlife Watching:**

- Discover Finland's diverse wildlife by embarking on wildlife watching excursions. Keep an eye out for native species such as brown bears, moose, wolves, lynx, and a variety of bird species in their natural habitats.

9. **Berry and Mushroom Picking:**

- Delight in the bounty of Finland's forests by foraging for wild berries and mushrooms. Join guided tours led by local experts who will help you identify edible species and share traditional recipes for cooking and preserving your harvest.

10. **Cultural Experiences:**

- Immerse yourself in Finnish culture by participating in traditional activities such as folk dancing, handicraft workshops, and visits to cultural heritage sites. Engage with locals, learn about Finnish traditions, and create lasting memories during your visit to Finland.

Whether you're seeking adrenaline-pumping adventures or serene nature experiences, Finland offers a wide range of activities to suit every traveler's interests and preferences. Explore the beauty of Finland's landscapes, immerse yourself in its rich culture, and create unforgettable memories during your stay in this enchanting Nordic country.

Hidden Facts

Fascinating Facts About Finland

1. **Sisu Mentality:**

   - Finland is known for its concept of "sisu," which roughly translates to resilience, determination, and perseverance in the face of adversity. This characteristic is deeply ingrained in Finnish culture and is often credited with helping Finland overcome challenges throughout its history.

2. **Everyman's Right:**

- Finland practices the concept of "Everyman's Right," which grants everyone the freedom to roam and enjoy the country's natural landscapes responsibly. This means that individuals have the right to access public and private lands for recreational activities such as hiking, camping, and berry picking, as long as they respect nature and property rights.

3. **Baby Boxes:**

- Finland is famous for its "baby boxes," a maternity package provided by the government to expectant mothers. The box contains essential baby items such as clothing, blankets, and diapers, as well as a cardboard box that doubles as a safe sleeping space for newborns. This initiative has contributed to Finland's low infant mortality rate and is considered a symbol of the country's commitment to social welfare.

4. **Coffee Consumption:**

- Finland holds the title of the world's top consumer of coffee per capita. Finnish coffee culture is deeply ingrained in daily life, with coffee breaks ("kahvitauko") being a cherished tradition in workplaces and social gatherings. Finns take their coffee seriously and often enjoy it strong and black, accompanied by sweet pastries or snacks.

5. **Innovative Education System:**

- Finland's education system consistently ranks among the best in the world, despite having minimal standardized testing and homework. Finnish schools emphasize creativity, critical thinking, and equality, with a focus on holistic development rather than rote memorization. Teachers are highly respected professionals, and education is free at all levels, including higher education.

6. **Design Capital:**

- Finland has a rich design heritage and is home to numerous iconic design brands and products. From furniture and textiles to architecture and technology, Finnish design is renowned for its simplicity, functionality, and timeless aesthetic. Helsinki, in particular, has earned a reputation as a design capital, with an abundance of design shops, galleries, and events.

7. **Summer Cottage Culture:**

- Finns have a deep connection to nature, and spending time at a summer cottage ("mökki") is a cherished tradition. Many Finns own or have access to a lakeside cottage, where they retreat to during the summer months to relax, unwind, and enjoy outdoor activities such as sauna bathing, swimming, fishing, and berry picking.

8. **Finnish Tango:**

- While tango may be associated with Argentina, Finland has its own unique style of tango known as "Finnish tango." Finnish tango is characterized by its melancholic melodies and heartfelt lyrics, reflecting themes of love, longing, and nostalgia. It has become an integral part of Finnish culture and is celebrated through music festivals, dance events, and competitions throughout the country.

9. **Moomins:**

- The Moomins, created by Finnish author Tove Jansson, are beloved characters that have captured the hearts of people around the world. These whimsical creatures inhabit the fictional Moominvalley and have become iconic symbols of Finnish culture. The Moomins have inspired books, comics, TV shows, movies, and even a theme park in Finland.

10. **Santa Claus' Post Office:**

- Finland is home to Santa Claus' main post office, located in the Arctic Circle town of Rovaniemi. Visitors can send letters to Santa Claus from all around the world, receive a special Arctic Circle postmark, and even meet Santa himself at Santa Claus Village. It's a magical destination that brings joy to visitors of all ages.

These hidden gems offer a glimpse into the unique and fascinating aspects of Finnish culture, traditions, and way of life. From the resilience of "sisu" to the whimsy of the Moomins, Finland has much to offer beyond its stunning landscapes and vibrant cities.

Local Events and Festivals

1. **Midsummer (Juhannus):**

- Midsummer is one of the most celebrated festivals in Finland, marking the longest day of the year and the beginning of summer. Traditional celebrations include lighting bonfires, dancing around maypoles, and enjoying outdoor activities with family and friends. It's a time when Finns retreat to their summer cottages to relax and unwind amidst nature.

2. **Helsinki Pride:**

- Helsinki Pride is an annual LGBTQ+ pride festival held in the Finnish capital, celebrating diversity, equality, and LGBTQ+ rights. The festival features a colorful parade, concerts, parties, film screenings, and cultural events aimed at

promoting   inclusion   and
acceptance.

3. **Ruisrock:**

- Ruisrock is one of Finland's largest
  and oldest rock music festivals, held
  annually on the island of Ruissalo
  near Turku. The festival attracts top
  international and Finnish artists
  across various genres, drawing
  music lovers from around the
  country and beyond.

4. **Flow Festival:**

- Flow Festival is a cutting-edge
  music and arts festival held in
  Helsinki, known for its eclectic
  lineup of artists, innovative art
  installations, and sustainable ethos.
  The festival showcases a diverse
  range of music genres, including
  indie rock, electronic, hip-hop, and

world music, alongside visual arts, film screenings, and food experiences.

5. **Savonlinna Opera Festival:**

- The Savonlinna Opera Festival is one of Finland's premier cultural events, held annually in the medieval Olavinlinna Castle in Savonlinna. The festival showcases world-class opera performances in a unique and atmospheric setting, attracting opera aficionados from around the world.

6. **Helsinki International Film Festival (Love & Anarchy):**

- Love & Anarchy is Finland's largest and most prestigious film festival, showcasing a diverse selection of international and Finnish films ranging from arthouse gems to mainstream hits. The festival features screenings, Q&A sessions with filmmakers, panel discussions, and special events celebrating the art of cinema.

7. Festival of Nine Lessons and Carols (Joulun ensimmäinen kuoro):

- The Festival of Nine Lessons and Carols is a beloved Christmas tradition in Finland, featuring a series of choral performances and readings recounting the story of Christmas. Held in churches and concert halls across the country, the festival captures the spirit of the holiday season with its beautiful music and festive atmosphere.

8. Pori Jazz:

- Pori Jazz is an internationally renowned jazz festival held annually in the coastal city of Pori. The festival attracts top jazz musicians from around the world, as well as artists from other genres such as blues, soul, and funk. With its diverse lineup and laid-back atmosphere, Pori Jazz is a highlight of Finland's summer festival season.

9. **Rovaniemi Christmas Market:**

- The Rovaniemi Christmas Market is a festive event held in the Arctic Circle town of Rovaniemi, known as the official hometown of Santa Claus. The market features traditional Finnish handicrafts, local delicacies, live performances, and, of course, a chance to meet Santa Claus himself in his enchanting Lapland home.

10. **Tampere Theatre Festival:**

- The Tampere Theatre Festival is one of the oldest and most prestigious theater festivals in Finland, showcasing a wide range of theatrical performances, from drama and comedy to experimental and avant-garde productions. The festival also hosts workshops, seminars, and discussions aimed at promoting dialogue and innovation in the performing arts.

These local events and festivals offer a glimpse into Finland's vibrant cultural scene, providing opportunities to celebrate, discover, and connect with the country's rich traditions, arts, and community spirit. Whether you're a music lover, art enthusiast, or simply looking to immerse yourself in Finnish culture, there's something for everyone to enjoy at these lively and memorable gatherings.

CHAPTER 6

ACCOMMODATION OPTIONS

1. Santa Claus Holiday Village

Address: Tahtikuja 2, Rovaniemi 96930
Finland

Phone: 009 358 40 0306273

About:

Luxurious cottage lodging awaits you at the Arctic Circle, nestled in the heart of Santa Claus Village. Their cabins boast top-notch amenities including private saunas, bathrooms, kitchenettes, and terraces, ensuring your utmost comfort. With just a short stroll from your cabin, you'll find yourself at Santa Claus Main Office in no time. Immerse yourself in a plethora of activities and excursions such as reindeer rides, husky dog sledging, snowmobile adventures, and more, all conveniently available within the village.

Property amenities

Sauna

Car hire
Taxi service

24-hour front desk

Room features

Flatscreen TV

Hair dryer

2. Wilderness Hotel Inari

Address: Inarintie 2, Inari 99870 Finland

About:

The Wilderness Hotel Inari sits beside the stunning Arctic wilderness lake, Lake Inari, offering breathtaking vistas and an optimal spot for observing the aurora. Their newest resort seamlessly blends comfort with a wilderness-themed style, accompanied by their renowned signature services. Located just five minutes from the attractions and amenities of Inari village, this premier resort provides the perfect fusion of high-quality lodging and pristine natural surroundings. With 12 Aurora Cabins, 40 wilderness rooms, and 8 log cabins, along with a Lappish-themed restaurant boasting panoramic views of Lake Inari, their resort offers distinctive accommodations. Whether it's summer or winter, Wilderness Hotel Inari serves as the perfect launching pad for your nature and aurora-related adventures—immerse yourself in the wild!

Property amenities

Sauna

Shuttle bus service

Room features

Flatscreen TV

Bath / shower

3. Arctic Light Hotel

Address: Valtakatu 18, Rovaniemi 96200 Finland

About:

Arctic Light Hotel in Rovaniemi is a top choice for travelers seeking a luxurious yet convenient stay. With amenities like free WiFi, a fitness center, and complimentary breakfast, guests enjoy comfort and convenience. The hotel's proximity to landmarks and dining options adds to its appeal. Overall, it's the perfect base for exploring Rovaniemi's attractions.

Property amenities

Car hire

24-hour check-in

Sauna

Room features

Flatscreen TV

4. Marski by Scandic

Address; Mannerheimintie 10, Helsinki 00100 Finland

Phone: 009 358 300 308400

About:

A contemporary lifestyle hotel in Helsinki, situated on the vibrant Mannerheimintie, offers a pleasant ambiance and an excellent location. With shopping streets, upscale boutiques, major attractions, and businesses nearby, guests enjoy easy access to everything Helsinki has to offer. The hotel underwent a full renovation in 2019, ensuring a modern and refreshed experience for guests.

Property amenities

24-hour check-in

Sauna

Yoga classes

24-hour front desk

Room features

Complimentary toiletries

Flatscreen TV

Bath / shower

Hair dryer

5. Hotel Haaga Central Park

Address: Nuijamiestentie 10, Helsinki 00320 Finland

About:

Experience first-class amenities and service at the BEST WESTERN PLUS Hotel Haaga in Helsinki, Finland. Conveniently located just 15 minutes from the city center and the airport, guests can enjoy nearby attractions like Central Park and Tali Golf Course. The hotel offers an on-site restaurant, indoor pool, sauna, and gym. Each guest room is well-appointed with broadband Internet and a mini-bar. Start your day with a complimentary full breakfast at this eco-friendly hotel.

Property amenities

Sauna

Room features

Walk-in shower

Complimentary toiletries

Hair dryer

Bidet

Room types

Non-smoking rooms

Family rooms

6. Wilderness Hotel Muotka

Address: Muotkantie 204, Saariselka 99830 Finland

About:

Wilderness Hotel Muotka is an ideal destination for honeymooners, anniversaries, or romantic escapes, offering a unique experience for those seeking an active holiday in a cozy and tranquil setting.

Property amenities

Sauna

Room features

Bath / shower

Complimentary toiletries

Hair dryer

7. Apukka Resort Rovaniemi

Address: Kiilopaantie 9 Kultaojantie, Saariselka 99830 Finland

Phone: 009 358 29 3700269

About:

Nestled in Rovaniemi, Lapland, our wilderness resort is a short 15-minute drive from Rovaniemi International Airport and Santa Claus Village. With unique Aurora accommodations like glass igloos and Lakeview Suites, they're an ideal spot for couples, families, or friends seeking a memorable getaway. Surrounded by Arctic nature, their resort offers prime opportunities for Northern Lights hunting and exciting excursions, including husky and reindeer tours. Enjoy delicious meals at their authentic Restaurant Aitta, featuring locally sourced ingredients. At Apukka Resort, you're welcomed like a cherished friend.

Property amenities

Shuttle bus service

Car hire

Taxi service

Sauna

Room features

Bidet

Walk-in shower

Bath / shower

Hair dryer

8. Valo Hotel & Work

Address: Mannerheimintie 109, Helsinki 00280 Finland

Phone: 009 358 10 3404000

About:

VALO Hotel & Work is a vibrant and welcoming hotel offering a blend of well-being, accommodation, and appealing workspaces with a Nordic influence. Situated centrally, nature is easily accessible, while the city's cultural offerings are just a short tram ride away. The hotel features a spacious indoor courtyard with a high glass roof, allowing sunlight to flood in, along with a roof terrace complete with log saunas and relaxation pools to enhance your experience.

Property amenities

24-hour check-in

24-hour front desk

Express check-in / check-out

Private check-in / check-out

Sauna

Car hire

Taxi service

Fitness / spa locker rooms

Room features

Cable / satellite TV

Bidet

Flatscreen TV

Walk-in shower

Complimentary toiletries

Hair dryer

9. Hotel Kultahippu

Address: Petsamontie 1, Ivalo 99800 Finland

About:

Hotel Kultahippu is situated in the heart of Ivalo, alongside the banks of the Ivalojoki River, offering immediate access to all amenities and the stunning natural surroundings. They offer comfortable accommodation, a variety of enticing dining options, and hospitable service to their guests. As a family-owned establishment, they pride themselves on providing a warm atmosphere. Welcome and unwind during your stay with them.

Property amenities

Sauna

Car hire

Room features

Flatscreen TV

Bath / shower

Hair dryer

10.   Arthur Hotel

Address: Vuorikatu 19, Helsinki 00100 Finland

About:

Arthur Hotel in Helsinki offers a quiet and convenient retreat for travelers, with comfortable rooms equipped with amenities like flat-screen TVs and free wifi. Guests can enjoy a sauna, complimentary breakfast, and easy access to top attractions and dining options in the city center. Whether traveling for business or leisure, Arthur Hotel promises a memorable stay in Helsinki.

Property amenities

Sauna

Taxi service

24-hour check-in

24-hour front desk

Room features

Flatscreen TV

Walk-in shower

Hair dryer

CHAPTER 7

WHERE TO EAT AND DRINK

1. Street Food Stands:

- Helsinki's Market Square (Kauppatori) is a great place to find street food stands offering Finnish delicacies such as salmon soup, reindeer meatballs, and cinnamon buns. You can also try traditional snacks like "karjalanpiirakka" (Karelian pasties) and "makkara" (Finnish sausage).

2. Market Halls:

- Market halls, such as Hakaniemi Market Hall in Helsinki and Kauppahalli in Tampere, are excellent destinations for sampling local produce, baked goods, and prepared foods. Enjoy a hearty lunch of Finnish specialties like "kalakukko" (fish pie) or "karjalanpaisti" (Karelian stew).

3. **Cafés and Bakeries:**

- Finland's cafés and bakeries are renowned for their delicious pastries, cakes, and coffee. Visit Café Esplanad in Helsinki for freshly baked cinnamon rolls, or try the "korvapuusti" (Finnish cinnamon bun) at Café Aino in Turku. Don't forget to pair your pastry with a cup of strong Finnish coffee.

4. **Traditional Restaurants:**

- For an authentic Finnish dining experience, head to traditional restaurants known as "ravintola" or "ravinteli." Sample Finnish classics such as "silli" (pickled herring), "poronkäristys" (sauteed reindeer), or "lohikeitto" (salmon soup) at restaurants like Savotta in Helsinki or Juuri in Turku.

5. **Food Trucks and Food Markets:**

- Keep an eye out for food trucks and food markets popping up in cities across Finland. From gourmet burgers to international cuisine, you'll find a diverse array of tasty treats on offer. Check out events like the "Street Food Thursday" market in Tampere or the "Food Market Helsinki" in Helsinki for a culinary adventure.

6. **Microbreweries and Craft Beer Bars:**

- Finland's craft beer scene has been booming in recent years, with microbreweries and craft beer bars popping up in cities and towns nationwide. Visit breweries like

Panimoravintola Bruuveri in Turku or Stadin Panimo in Helsinki to sample locally brewed beers in a cozy atmosphere.

7. **Saloons and Pubs:**

- Finnish saloons and pubs offer a laid-back atmosphere to enjoy a drink with friends or watch live sports events. Head to Olutravintola Pikkulintu in Helsinki for a wide selection of craft beers, or visit the Old Bank Wine Bar in Turku for a cozy wine tasting experience.

8. **Sámi Restaurants:**

- In Lapland, you'll find restaurants specializing in Sámi cuisine, featuring traditional dishes made from reindeer, fish, and wild herbs. Visit SámiSoster in Rovaniemi or

Sámi Duodji in Inari to savor the flavors of the Arctic.

9. **Vegan and Vegetarian Restaurants:**

- Finland's culinary scene caters to vegans and vegetarians with an increasing number of restaurants offering plant-based options. Check out restaurants like Yes Yes Yes in Helsinki or Gopal in Tampere for innovative vegan and vegetarian dishes.

10. **Food Tours and Culinary Experiences:**

- Join a guided food tour or culinary experience to discover the best of Finnish cuisine and local specialties. Companies like Food Sightseeing Helsinki and Taste of Helsinki offer guided tours, tastings, and cooking classes led by knowledgeable locals.

From street food stalls to fine dining restaurants, Finland offers a wide range of culinary experiences to suit every taste and budget. Whether you're craving traditional Finnish dishes, international cuisine, or craft beer and cocktails, you'll find plenty of delicious options to explore throughout the country.

Some of the restaurants are:

1. Spis

Location and contact

Kasarmikatu 26, Helsinki 00130 Finland

0.3 miles from The Esplanadi Park

+358 45 3051211

Details

CUISINES

European, Scandinavian

SPECIAL DIETS

Vegetarian Friendly, Vegan Options, Gluten Free Options

MEALS

Dinner

ABOUT

Delicious food, made with fresh ingredients, and served with warm hospitality. Wine prices are reasonable.

2. Baskeri & Basso

Location and contact

Tehtaankatu 27-29, Helsinki 00150 Finland

+358 50 4673400

Details

SPECIAL DIETS

Vegetarian Friendly, Vegan Options, Gluten Free Options

MEALS

Dinner

CUISINES

European, Central European

FEATURES

Reservations, Seating, Wheelchair Accessible, Serves Alcohol, Full Bar, Accepts Credit Cards, Table Service

3. Gran Delicato

Location and contact

Kalevankatu 34/Albertinkatu 31, Helsinki 00180 Finland

Kampinmalmi

+358 50 5135007

Details

CUISINES

Greek, Cafe, Mediterranean, European, Healthy

SPECIAL DIETS

Vegetarian Friendly, Gluten Free Options, Vegan Options

MEALS

Lunch, Breakfast

FEATURES

Takeout, Reservations, Seating, Accepts Credit Cards, Table Service, Serves Alcohol, Free Wifi, Gift Cards Available

4. Finlandia Caviar

Location and contact

Etelaranta 20, Helsinki 00130 Finland

0.3 miles from The Esplanadi Park

+358 10 5817810

Details

About:

Finlandia Caviar stands out as the first caviar shop in Helsinki, offering an extensive collection of roes and caviars, and renowned as one of Finland's premier oyster restaurants. As a family-owned business, they're recognized as experts in luxury seafood products. their commitment to quality extends to sourcing the freshest seafood from trusted suppliers. Visitors and locals alike prioritize their shop and restaurant, which boasts Scandinavian winter-inspired decor and elegant furnishings. Experience their 5-star style and be amazed at Finlandia Caviar Shop & Restaurant.

PRICE RANGE
$11 - $107
CUISINES
Seafood, European, Scandinavian
MEALS
Dinner, Late Night, Drinks
FEATURES
Gift Cards Available, Reservations, Seating, Serves Alcohol, Accepts American Express, Accepts Mastercard, Accepts Visa, Free Wifi, Accepts Discover, Accepts Credit Cards, Table Service, Street Parking, Wine and Beer, Digital Payments, Waterfront, Beach, Dog Friendly, Non-smoking restaurants

5. Rioni Helsinki

Location and contact

Kasarmikatu 25, Helsinki 00130 Finland

0.1 miles from The Esplanadi Park

+358 50 5512264

Details:

About:

Immerse yourself in an authentic Georgian atmosphere right here in Helsinki. Their restaurant offers original recipes, imported wines, and genuine hospitality to transport you to the heart of Georgia. Indulge in versatile meals meant for sharing, complemented by beautiful design. And for a touch of summer, their warm inner courtyard awaits year-round. Experience the real deal, their pride and joy—a truly authentic Georgian restaurant in the heart of Helsinki.

PRICE RANGE
$6 - $64
CUISINES
Georgian, Eastern European, International
SPECIAL DIETS
Vegetarian Friendly, Vegan Options, Gluten Free Options
MEALS
Lunch, Dinner, Brunch, Late Night, Drinks
FEATURES
Takeout, Reservations, Seating, Serves Alcohol, Full Bar, Table Service, Highchairs Available, Wheelchair Accessible, Wine and Beer, Dog Friendly, Family style, Non-smoking restaurants, Gift Cards Available

6. Olo Ravintola

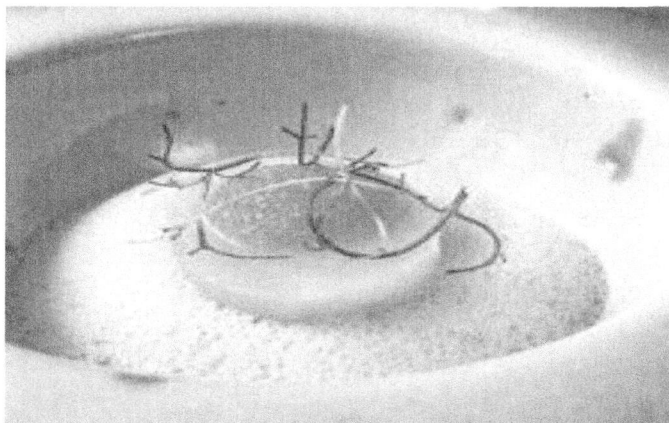

Location and contact

Pohjoisesplanadi 5, Helsinki 00170 Finland

Vironniemi

0.2 miles from Helsinki Cathedral

+358 10 3206250

Details

About:
Situated by the Market Square in Helsinki, Olo is renowned for its cuisine crafted by Tuomas Vierelä and its welcoming service. Housed in a building with over 200 years of history, this beautiful restaurant specializes in creating

insightful taste sensations from Scandinavian ingredients and has held a Michelin star since 2011. At Olo, everything exudes joy and an unwavering passion for crafting unique dining experiences. It's no surprise that Olo's dinner menu is a must-try for food enthusiasts. Additionally, Garden by Olo offers delightful taste sensations for groups with reservations. They invite you to savor memorable experiences with them!

PRICE RANGE
$128 - $181
CUISINES
Contemporary, Scandinavian
SPECIAL DIETS
Vegetarian Friendly, Vegan Options, Gluten Free Options
MEALS
Dinner, Drinks
FEATURES
Seating, Highchairs Available, Wheelchair Accessible, Serves Alcohol, Full Bar, Accepts American Express, Accepts Mastercard, Accepts Visa, Free Wifi, Reservations, Private Dining, Accepts Credit Cards, Table Service

7. Ravintola Kuu

Location and contact

Toolonkatu 27, Helsinki 00260 Finland

Taka-Toolo

0.5 miles from Temppeliaukio Church

+358 9 27090973

Details

About:

Finnish Restaurant Kuu, named after "the Moon," was

established in 1966 with a vision reaching beyond the

clouds. Since its inception, the atmosphere has been likened to that of a continental bistro. Their kitchen presents a variety of Finnish classics and Scandinavian dishes with a contemporary twist. They prioritize the use of the finest ingredients, highlighting their natural flavors with a simple yet balanced aesthetic. Featuring a wealth of Finnish fish, meat, berries, and seasonal vegetables, they invite you to indulge in a culinary journey with them.

PRICE RANGE
$11 - $55
CUISINES
European, Scandinavian
SPECIAL DIETS
Vegetarian Friendly, Vegan Options, Gluten Free Options
MEALS
Lunch, Dinner, Late Night, Drinks
FEATURES
Reservations, Seating, Highchairs Available, Serves Alcohol, Full Bar, Free Wifi, Accepts Credit Cards, Table Service, Wine and Beer, Gift Cards Available

CHAPTER 8

WHERE TO SHOP AND WHAT TO BUY

1. **Market Squares:**

   - **Locations:** Market squares, such as Helsinki's Market Square (Kauppatori) and Turku's Old Great Square (Vanha Suurtori), are bustling hubs where you can find fresh produce, local handicrafts, and souvenirs. Look for vendors selling berries, mushrooms, handmade textiles, and traditional Finnish goods.

2. **Design Districts:**

   - **Locations:** Helsinki's Design District and Turku's Old Great Square are known for their concentration of design shops, boutiques, and galleries. Explore streets like Esplanadi and Aleksanterinkatu in Helsinki or Aurakatu and Linnankatu in Turku to discover Finnish design treasures, including Marimekko textiles, Iittala glassware, and Artek furniture.

3. **Craft Markets and Fairs:**

- **Locations:** Keep an eye out for craft markets and fairs held in cities and towns across Finland, especially during the summer months. These events showcase the work of local artisans and craftsmen, offering a wide range of handmade products such as pottery, ceramics, jewelry, and woodcarvings.

4. **Shopping Malls and Department Stores:**

- **Locations:** Finland's major cities are home to modern shopping malls and department stores where you can find a variety of goods under one roof. Visit malls like Kamppi and Forum in Helsinki or Ratina and Koskikeskus in Tampere for clothing, electronics, home goods, and more.

5. **Flea Markets and Secondhand Shops:**

- **Locations:** Browse through flea markets and secondhand shops scattered throughout Finland to uncover unique vintage finds and preloved treasures. Check out places like Hietalahti Market Hall Flea Market in Helsinki or

Kierrätyskeskus in Tampere for eclectic items at bargain prices.

6. **Specialty Food Stores:**

   - **Locations:** Explore specialty food stores and delicatessens to sample and purchase Finnish culinary delights. Look for stores like Stockmann's Food Market Hall in Helsinki or Tampere Market Hall in Tampere for gourmet cheeses, smoked fish, reindeer products, and other Finnish delicacies.

7. **Arts and Crafts Villages:**

   - **Locations:** Visit arts and crafts villages, such as Fiskars Village in Southern Finland or Iittala Village in Hämeenlinna, to discover unique handmade goods and artisanal products. These picturesque villages are home to workshops, studios, and shops showcasing Finnish craftsmanship at its finest.

8. Outdoor Markets and Bazaars:

- **Locations:** Experience the vibrant atmosphere of outdoor markets and bazaars held in various cities and towns throughout Finland. From the Santa Claus Village in Rovaniemi to the Tampere Market Square, these markets offer a wide range of goods, including local crafts, clothing, souvenirs, and food.

9. Antique Shops and Galleries:

- **Locations:** Antique shops and galleries are scattered across Finland, offering antique furniture, vintage clothing, retro decor, and collectible items. Explore neighborhoods like Punavuori in Helsinki or Martti in Turku for a glimpse into Finland's rich history and cultural heritage.

10.   **Christmas Markets:**

- **Locations:** During the holiday season, Christmas markets pop up in cities and towns across Finland, offering festive decorations, handicrafts, and traditional Finnish treats. Visit markets like the Helsinki Christmas Market or the Turku Christmas Market to shop for unique gifts and soak up the holiday spirit.

From traditional markets to modern malls, Finland offers a diverse shopping experience with something for everyone to enjoy. Whether you're looking for designer goods, artisanal crafts, or tasty treats, you'll find plenty of opportunities to shop and discover Finnish culture and creativity throughout the country.

CHAPTER 9

TRAVEL INFORMATION FOR FINLAND

1. Total Budget for Travel:

- The total budget for traveling to Finland can vary depending on factors such as the duration of your stay, accommodation preferences, dining habits, and planned activities. As a rough estimate, budget travelers may aim for around €50-100 per day, while mid-range travelers may budget €100-200 per day. This budget should cover accommodation, meals, transportation, sightseeing, and incidental expenses.

2. Visa Information:

- Finland is a member of the Schengen Area, which allows citizens of certain countries to enter Finland visa-free for short stays of up to 90 days within a 180-day period. Citizens of Schengen Area countries, EU/EEA countries, and several other countries do not need a visa for short visits to Finland.

- Travelers from countries outside the Schengen Area may need to apply for a Schengen visa before their trip. The visa application process typically requires providing proof of travel arrangements, accommodation bookings, financial means, travel insurance, and a valid passport. It's essential to check the visa requirements specific to your nationality and planned duration of stay in Finland.

3. Embassy Information:

If you need assistance while in Finland, you can contact your country's embassy or consulate for consular services and support. Here are some embassy details:

United States Embassy in Finland

- Address: Itäinen Puistotie 14B, 00140 Helsinki, Finland
- Phone: +358 9 616250
- Website: https://fi.usembassy.gov/

United Kingdom Embassy in Finland

- Address: Itäinen Puistotie 17, 00140 Helsinki, Finland
- Phone: +358 9 2286 5100
- Website: https://www.gov.uk/world/organisations/british-embassy-helsinki

Embassy of Canada to Finland

- Address: Mariankatu 5 B, 3rd floor, 00170 Helsinki, Finland
- Phone: +358 9 228 530
- Website: https://www.canadainternational.gc.ca/finland-finlande/

4. Budget Planner:

To help plan your finances for your trip to Finland, consider creating a budget planner. Start by listing all expected expenses, including:

- Accommodation: Estimate the cost of accommodation per night based on your preferred type of lodging (hostel, hotel, Airbnb, etc.) and multiply it by the number of nights you plan to stay.
- Transportation: Include expenses for flights, train or bus tickets, rental cars, and local transportation (such as public transit passes or taxi fares).

- Meals: Estimate daily meal costs based on your dining preferences (eating out at restaurants, cooking your meals, etc.).
- Activities: Budget for sightseeing tours, museum entrance fees, outdoor activities, and any other experiences you plan to participate in.
- Miscellaneous: Set aside funds for souvenirs, shopping, unexpected expenses, and emergencies.

Once you have listed all expenses, tally up the total to determine your estimated travel budget. Compare this total to your available funds to ensure that you can afford your trip comfortably. Adjust your budget as needed to stay within your financial means while still enjoying your travel experience in Finland. See sample attached below:

TRAVEL BUDGET PLANNER

Travel Budget

Destination :

Travel Dates :

Details	Estimated	Actual
Accomodation		
Transportation		
Meals		
Activities		
Miscellaneous		

Notes

Travel Budget

Destination :		Travel Dates :

Details	Estimated	Actual
Accomodation		
Transportation		
Meals		
Activities		
Miscellaneous		

Notes

Travel Budget

Destination :		Travel Dates :

Details	Estimated	Actual
Accomodation		
Transportation		
Meals		
Activities		
Miscellaneous		

Notes

Itinerary for Exploring Finland

Day 1: Arrival in Helsinki

- Arrive in Helsinki, Finland's vibrant capital city.

- Check into your accommodation and freshen up.

- Explore the city center, starting with Senate Square and Helsinki Cathedral.

- Visit the bustling Market Square (Kauppatori) and sample local delicacies.

- Take a stroll along the waterfront and admire the iconic Helsinki Design District.

- Enjoy dinner at a traditional Finnish restaurant.

Day 2: Helsinki Highlights

- Begin your day with a visit to Suomenlinna Sea Fortress, a UNESCO World Heritage Site.

- Explore the Helsinki City Museum and learn about the city's history and culture.

- Wander through the charming streets of the Kallio and Punavuori districts.

- Visit the Ateneum Art Museum to admire Finnish and international artwork.

- Spend the evening relaxing in a traditional Finnish sauna.

Day 3: Turku and Archipelago Adventure

- Travel to Turku, Finland's oldest city, located on the southwest coast.

- Explore Turku Castle, one of Finland's most significant historical landmarks.

- Take a cruise through the picturesque Turku Archipelago and admire the stunning scenery.

- Visit the Turku Market Square and enjoy lunch at a local cafe.

- Explore the Turku Cathedral and stroll along the Aura River.

Day 4: Tampere and Lakeland Excursion

- Journey to Tampere, known as the "Manchester of Finland," located in the heart of the Finnish Lakeland.

- Explore the vibrant city center and visit attractions such as the Moomin Museum and Nasinneula Observation Tower.

- Enjoy a leisurely boat cruise on Lake Pyhäjärvi and soak in the tranquil surroundings.

- Explore the Pyynikki Ridge and enjoy panoramic views of Tampere from the observation tower.

- Sample local cuisine at a traditional Finnish restaurant in Tampere.

Day 5: Rovaniemi and Arctic Adventure

- Fly or take a train to Rovaniemi, the gateway to Finnish Lapland.

- Visit the Santa Claus Village and meet Santa Claus himself.

- Explore the Arktikum Science Centre and Museum to learn about the Arctic region.

- Enjoy outdoor activities such as husky sledding, reindeer sleigh rides, or snowmobiling.

- Spend the evening searching for the Northern Lights in the Arctic wilderness.

Day 6: Wilderness Retreat and Sauna Experience

- Embark on a wilderness retreat in the Finnish Lapland and reconnect with nature.

- Explore the pristine wilderness on a guided hike or snowshoeing excursion.

- Enjoy a traditional Finnish sauna experience, followed by a dip in a refreshing ice hole or a snowbank.

- Relax by the fireplace and enjoy a hearty Finnish meal prepared with local ingredients.

- Spend the night in a cozy wilderness cabin or glass igloo and marvel at the starry night sky.

Day 7: Departure from Finland

- Enjoy a leisurely breakfast at your accommodation.

- Take one last stroll through the Finnish wilderness or explore the local surroundings.

- Transfer to the airport or train station for your departure from Finland.

- Bid farewell to the Land of a Thousand Lakes, taking with you cherished memories of your Finnish adventure.

Photography Tips for Capturing Finland's Beauty

1. **Golden Hour Magic:**

   - Take advantage of Finland's long summer days and short winter days to capture stunning golden hour light. The soft, warm glow during sunrise and sunset adds a magical touch to landscapes and cityscapes.

2. **Seasonal Spectacles:**

   - Capture the unique beauty of Finland's changing seasons, from the vibrant colors of autumn foliage to the snowy landscapes of winter and the midnight sun of summer.

Each season offers its own photographic opportunities and challenges, so be prepared to adapt your shooting techniques accordingly.

3. **Embrace the Elements:**

- Don't let Finland's unpredictable weather deter you from capturing breathtaking images. Embrace the elements and use them to your advantage, whether it's capturing the drama of storm clouds rolling in or the tranquility of snow-covered landscapes.

4. **Focus on Details:**

- Look beyond the sweeping vistas and focus on capturing the smaller details that make Finland special. Whether it's the intricate patterns of snowflakes, the textures of tree bark, or the reflections in a glassy lake, paying attention to details can result in compelling and intimate photographs.

5. **Seek Unique Perspectives:**

- Experiment with different angles, compositions, and perspectives to create visually interesting photographs. Get down low to capture reflections in water, shoot from high vantage points for sweeping views, or use leading lines to draw the viewer's eye into the scene.

6. **Include People for Scale:**

- Adding human elements to your photographs can help provide a sense of scale and perspective, especially when photographing vast landscapes or towering landmarks.

Consider including people in your shots to add context and storytelling to your images.

7. **Capture Local Culture:**

- Don't forget to capture the essence of Finnish culture and traditions through your photographs. Whether it's candid portraits of locals, snapshots of traditional architecture, or scenes from local festivals and events, documenting the cultural aspects of Finland can add depth and richness to your photo collection.

8. **Experiment with Long Exposures:**

- Experiment with long exposure photography to capture the movement of clouds, waterfalls, or Northern Lights. Use a tripod to keep your camera steady and adjust your exposure settings to achieve the desired effect, whether it's smooth, flowing water or streaks of light in the night sky.

9. **Stay Patient and Observant:**

Great photographs often require patience and observation. Take the time to scout locations, wait for the right light, and observe your surroundings for interesting compositions and moments worth capturing. Don't be afraid to wait for the perfect moment to click the shutter.

10. **Tell a Story:**

Use your photographs to tell a story about your experience in Finland. Whether it's a series of images documenting a day in the life of a Finnish fisherman, the journey of a reindeer herder, or the beauty of a winter wonderland, let your photos convey the unique stories and experiences you encounter during your travels in Finland.

CHAPTER 10

DEALING WITH EMERGENCIES

1. Emergency Services:

- In case of an emergency, dial 112 to reach emergency services in Finland. This number can be used to request assistance from the police, fire department, ambulance, or other emergency services.

2. Medical Assistance:

- If you require medical assistance, Finland has a comprehensive healthcare system with hospitals, clinics, and medical professionals available throughout the country. In non-life-threatening situations, you can visit a local health center (terveysasema) for medical care.

3. **Pharmacies:**

- Pharmacies (apteekki) in Finland provide medications, over-the-counter remedies, and healthcare advice. In case of minor illnesses or injuries, you can visit a pharmacy for assistance. Pharmacists are knowledgeable and can recommend suitable treatments for common ailments.

4. **Language Assistance:**

- If you require assistance but do not speak Finnish or Swedish, Finland's emergency services and healthcare providers often have English-speaking staff available to assist you. You can also ask for assistance from a local or fellow traveler who speaks your language.

5. **Lost or Stolen Documents:**

- If your passport, identification, or other important documents are lost or stolen, contact the nearest police station to report the incident. They can provide assistance and guidance on the necessary steps to take, including obtaining a replacement document from your embassy or consulate.

6. **Natural Disasters:**

- Finland is generally safe from major natural disasters such as earthquakes, hurricanes, or tsunamis. However, extreme weather conditions such as heavy snowfall or forest fires can occur, especially in certain regions. Stay up-to-date on weather forecasts and follow any instructions or warnings issued by local authorities.

7. **Safety Precautions:**

- Take common-sense safety precautions to avoid emergencies while traveling in Finland. This includes staying hydrated, wearing appropriate clothing for the weather conditions, being cautious when participating in outdoor activities, and following safety guidelines for activities such as hiking, skiing, or boating.

8. **Travel Insurance:**

- It's advisable to have travel insurance that covers medical emergencies, trip cancellations, and other unforeseen circumstances while traveling in Finland. Make sure you understand the terms and coverage of your insurance policy and carry the necessary documentation with you during your trip.

9. **Consular Assistance:**

- If you encounter serious difficulties while in Finland, such as legal issues, accidents, or emergencies, you can contact your country's embassy or consulate for assistance. They can provide consular services, support, and guidance to citizens in need.

10. **Emergency Preparedness:**

- Familiarize yourself with emergency procedures and resources available in Finland before your trip. This includes knowing the location of emergency exits, first aid kits, and fire extinguishers in your accommodation, as well as any emergency contact information provided by your hotel or lodging.

By being prepared and knowing how to respond in case of emergencies, you can ensure a safe and enjoyable experience while traveling in Finland. Remember to stay calm, assess the situation carefully, and seek assistance from local authorities or healthcare professionals as needed.

CONCLUSION

In conclusion, Finland is a captivating destination offering a blend of natural beauty, cultural richness, and modern sophistication. From the vibrant cities of Helsinki, Turku, and Tampere to the pristine wilderness of Lapland, Finland has something to offer every traveler.

Throughout this travel guide, we've explored the diverse landscapes, vibrant culture, and unique experiences that Finland has to offer. From the enchanting Northern Lights and the magical Midnight Sun to the rich history and traditions of the Finnish people, Finland is a country that never fails to leave a lasting impression on its visitors.

Whether you're seeking outdoor adventures like hiking, skiing, and snowboarding, or indulging in cultural delights such as sauna rituals, traditional cuisine, and design shopping, Finland offers endless opportunities for exploration and discovery.

As you embark on your journey to Finland, we hope this guide serves as a valuable resource, providing insights, tips, and recommendations to help you make the most of your travel experience. Whether you're a first-time visitor or a seasoned traveler, Finland promises unforgettable moments and lifelong memories waiting to be made.

So pack your bags, embrace the spirit of adventure, and immerse yourself in the beauty and wonder of Finland. From the northernmost reaches of Lapland to the southern shores of the Baltic Sea, let Finland's charm and allure captivate your heart and soul as you embark on an unforgettable journey of discovery and delight.

TRAVEL JOURNAL
Weekly check in

DATE _____

TOP 3 PLACES TO VISIT THIS WEEK

1 _____

2 _____

3 _____

MOST REWARDING INTERACTION I
HAD THIS WEEK

THIS WEEK I FELT

NEXT WEEK I WANT TO

_____

_____

_____

_____

THINGS I ACCOMPLISHED THIS
WEEK

THINGS I WILL LOVE TO SHARE
WITH MY...

MY RANKING OF THE WEEK

☆ ☆ ☆ ☆ ☆

TRAVEL JOURNAL

Weekly check in

DATE _____

TOP 3 PLACES TO VISIT THIS WEEK

1 _____

2 _____

3 _____

MOST REWARDING INTERACTION I
HAD THIS WEEK

THIS WEEK I FELT

NEXT WEEK I WANT TO _____

_____

_____

_____

THINGS I ACCOMPLISHED THIS
WEEK

THINGS I WILL LOVE TO SHARE
WITH MY...

MY RANKING OF THE WEEK

☆ ☆ ☆ ☆ ☆

TRAVEL JOURNAL
Weekly check in

DATE

TOP 3 PLACES TO VISIT THIS WEEK

1

2

3

MOST REWARDING INTERACTION I HAD THIS WEEK

THIS WEEK I FELT

NEXT WEEK I WANT TO

THINGS I ACCOMPLISHED THIS WEEK

THINGS I WILL LOVE TO SHARE WITH MY...

MY RANKING OF THE WEEK

☆ ☆ ☆ ☆ ☆

TRAVEL JOURNAL
Weekly check in

DATE _____

TOP 3 PLACES TO VISIT THIS WEEK

1 _____

2 _____

3 _____

MOST REWARDING INTERACTION I
HAD THIS WEEK
_____

THIS WEEK I FELT

NEXT WEEK I WANT TO _____

_____

_____

_____

_____

THINGS I ACCOMPLISHED THIS
WEEK

THINGS I WILL LOVE TO SHARE
WITH MY...

MY RANKING OF THE WEEK
☆ ☆ ☆ ☆ ☆

TRAVEL JOURNAL

Weekly check in

DATE _____

TOP 3 PLACES TO VISIT THIS WEEK

1 _____

2 _____

3 _____

MOST REWARDING INTERACTION I
HAD THIS WEEK

THIS WEEK I FELT

NEXT WEEK I WANT TO _____

_____

_____

_____

THINGS I ACCOMPLISHED THIS
WEEK

THINGS I WILL LOVE TO SHARE
WITH MY...

MY RANKING OF THE WEEK

☆ ☆ ☆ ☆ ☆

Dear reader,

Thank you for choosing this travel guide to Finland. We hope you found it informative and inspiring. If you enjoyed your experience, please consider leaving positive feedback on the book's page. Safe travels and happy exploring!

Printed in Great Britain
by Amazon

42594402R00086